SCALA

PROGRAMMING

LEARN SCALA
PROGRAMMING
FAST AND EASY

By Matthew Gimson

Table of Contents

Disclaimer

While all attempts have been made to verify the information provided in this book, the author does assume any responsibility for errors, omissions, or contrary interpretations of the subject matter contained within. **The information provided in this book is for educational and entertainment purposes only. The reader is responsible for his or her own actions and the author does not accept any responsibilities for any liabilities or damages, real or perceived, resulting from the use of this information.**

The trademarks that are used are without any consent, and the publication of the trademark is without permission or backing by the trademark owner. All trademarks and brands within this book are for clarifying purposes only and are the owned by the owners themselves, not affiliated with this document.

Chapter 1- Definition

Scala is one of a few modern programming languages which support numerous programming paradigms. The language was developed to provide programmers with a common programming pattern in a type-safe, elegant, and concise manner. The first version of this programming language was created in the year 2003 by Martin Odersky. The language is well known for its ability to integrate the functional and object-oriented features in a smooth manner.

The language is known for using constructs which are closely related to those used in Java and has a wide range of supported features, making it a very useful programming language. Most of the libraries used in Scala and those used in Java are interchangeable, making Scala very easy to learn for those already familiar with the Java language. This shows how close the two languages are to one another. For those who are good in programming languages such as C and C++, you will also find it easy to learn Scala programming language.

Due to the language's ability to supports the use of functions and it's strong type system, programs written in this language are small in size compared to those written in general-purpose programming languages. Most design decisions for this programming language were made to cover the weaknesses associated with the Java programming language. The source code for this programming language should be transformed into the

Java byte code after compilation, so that it can be executable on the Java virtual machine (JVM). It is possible for the programmer to make use of libraries which belong to Java while programming in Scala, and the opposite is also true. However, the functional programming used in Scala seems advanced compared to what we find in Java. It uses the curly-brace syntax similar to what is used in C programming.

This system type is also much more advanced as it supports data types including algebraic expressions, anonymous types and higher-order types. This shows how interesting and important it is for you to learn this programming language.

Chapter 2- Setting up the Environment

The Scala programming language can be installed on any Windows-like or UNIX-like operating system. However, your computer should first be installed with Java 1.5 or above before installing Scala, otherwise, you will encounter errors when you try installing.

Installation of Scala on Windows

Installing Java- we have already mentioned that Java must be installed first. Begin be adding the environment variable for "*JAVA_HOME*" and then add the directory of the JDK bin to the "*PATH*" variable. If you need to verify whether this worked successfully, just open the Windows command prompt and run the command "*java -version*". You should get the following output:

```
C:\>java -version
java version "1.6.0_15"
Java(TM) SE Runtime Environment (build 1.6.0_15-b03)
Java HotSpot(TM) 64-Bit Server VM (build 14.1-b02, mixed mode)

C:\>
```

Once you have succeeded in the above step, you should verify whether or not the Java compiler is installed on your system.

Again, on Windows' command prompt, run the command "*javac –version*" and observed the output. If it is installed, the output should be as follows:

```
C:\>javac -version
javac 1.6.0_15

C:\>
```

Once you get the above output, and then know that you are set.

Setting up Scala- you can then download Scala from online for installation on your system. After the download, put the setup file in the "*C:/>*" directory. Make sure you are logged in with admin privileges so that you will be in a position to perform the installation. After that, just open the command prompt and run the command "*java -jar scala-2.9.0.1-installer.jar*". This is shown below:

```
C:\>java -jar scala-2.9.0.1-installer.jar

C:\>
```

An installation wizard will be presented and this will guide you through the installation process. You will be prompted to accept the license, do so and specify the path where the installation should be done. Once this process is done, verify whether it was successful by opening the command prompt and running the command "*scala – version*". This is shown below:

```
C:\>scala -version
Scala code runner version 2.9.0.1 -- Copyright 2002-2011
```

The figure shows that the installation was successful and you are set to start programming.

Installation of Scala on Linux and Mac OS X

Setting up Java- before beginning the installation process, you must have installed JDK 1.5 or above on your computer and set up the Java environment variable. The directory of the JDK bin should also be added to the *"PATH"* variable. To verify whether this is already set up open the command prompt and execute the command *"java –version"*. The output should be as follows:

```
$java -version
java version "1.5.0_22"
Java(TM) 2 Runtime Environment, Standard Edition (build 1.5.0_22-b03)
Java HotSpot(TM) Server VM (build 1.5.0_22-b03, mixed mode)
$
```

If you see the above output then you know that everything is okay. You now need to check whether the Java compiler has been installed on the computer. Just open the command prompt and then execute the command *"javac –version"*. The output should be as follows:

```
$javac -version
javac 1.5.0_22
javac: no source files
Usage: javac <options> <source files>
```

Setting up Scala- the next step is to download Scala. This is available online for free download. After the download, put it in your *"/tmp"* directory. Make sure that you are logged into the system with admin privileges before proceeding. Open the command prompt and run the command *"java -jar scala-2.9.0.1-installer.jar"*. This is shown below:

```
$java -jar scala-2.9.0.1-installer.jar
Welcome to the installation of scala 2.9.0.1!
The homepage is at: http://scala-lang.org/
press 1 to continue, 2 to quit, 3 to redisplay
1
.............................................
[ Starting to unpack ]
[ Processing package: Software Package Installation (1/1) ]
[ Unpacking finished ]
[ Console installation done ]
```

You will be asked to accept the license for the software. Accept by typing 1 on the prompt. You will then be asked to specify the path for the installation to be done. Once the process of installation is over, open the command prompt and then type the command "*scala —version*" and press the "*Enter*" key. This will verify whether the installation was successful. You should see the following:

```
$scala -version
Scala code runner version 2.9.0.1 -- Copyright 2002-2011
```

If you see the output shown in the above figure, you have successfully installed Scala on your system. You are now set to begin programming

Chapter 3- Scala Basic Syntax

Most of the constructs in this language are closely related to the ones in Java. The big difference between the two is that in Scala it is optional for you to use the line end character. A Scala program is made up of objects with methods, and the objects communicate by invoking each other's methods.

Interactive Mode Programming in Scala

We can run Scala scripts on the command prompt rather than having to create a file. Just open the command prompt and then type the command "*scala*". This is shown in the figure below:

```
C:\>scala
Welcome to Scala version 2.9.0.1
Type in expressions to have them evaluated.
Type :help for more information.

scala>
```

As shown in the above figure, the command prompt for the programming language has been presented to you after executing the command. Let us demonstrate how to run scripts on this prompt. Type the following on the prompt and then hit the *"Enter"* key:

print("Hello there!);

After hitting the *"Enter"* key, you will observe the following output:

Hello there!

As you can see, we get the text which we specified above as the output. That is how interactive mode programming works in this programming language. We just run our commands on the Scala command prompt.

Script Mode programming in Scala

This involves writing the code in a file and then saving it. The code is compiled in the file and then executed. Let us demonstrate how this is done.

Open your text editor, such as Notepad, and then add the following code:

```
objectHelloThere{
/* My first program in Scala
 * The text "Hello there!" should be printed as the output
*/
def main(args:Array[String]){
println("Hello there!")// prints Hello there!
}
}
```

Once you have added the above code to your file, just save it with the name *"Hello.scala"*. Make sure that you save it in a directory which you can easily access. After that, open the command prompt and then navigate to the directory where you saved the file. Once you are there, type the command *"scalacHello.scala"*. Note that the last name of the command is the name of our file, so if you used a different name, then use that name rather than the one we have used here.

The command is aimed at compiling our source code which we saved in the file. If there are errors in the code, you will be notified of this, however, if your program is okay, then several other files will be generated in the directory. One of the files will be named *"Hello.class"*, and this contains the byte code to be executed on the Java virtual machine. We now need to execute the program. Just type the command *"scala Hello"* on the same command prompt and then hit the *"Enter"* key. You will observe the text *"Hello there!"* printed on your window.

Comments in Scala

With Scala, comments can be either single line or block comments. This is similar to what we find in Java. If the comments take up several lines, they can be nested, but this should be done in a specific way. What happens is that if the Scala compiler meets characters placed in a comment, then it will ignore and skip them, meaning they will have no effect on your program. This is shown in the code below:

```
objectHelloThere{
/* My first program in Scala
* The text "Hello there!" will be printed as the output.

* An example of Scala multi-line comments.
*/
def main(args:Array[String]){
// Prints Hello there
// A single line comment in scala
println("Hello there!")
}
}
```

You are now are of how to denote both the single-line and multi-line comments in Scala.

Chapter 4- Variables in Scala

In Scala, variables refer to memory locations which are used for storage of values. This indicates that once a variable is created, a memory space for the same is reserved. A variable should belong to one of the data types supported in Scala. This means that the amount of space which is reserved for the variable is equal to the amount of memory which is needed for the variable of that particular data type. By using variables we can store values of different data types such as integers, characters, long, double and string.

Variable Declaration

Scala has its own way on way that variables can be declared. It is possible for us to assign a value to the variable during the time of declaration. The variable can also be a constant, in which case it will impossible for its value to be changed. The *"var"* keyword can be used for declaration of variables in Scala. This is shown below:

var name :String="John"

What we have done is that we have used the *"var"* keyword to declare a variable which we have the name *"name"*.

This is an indication that it is a variable and that its value can be changed to something else. This kind of variable is called a "*mutable variable*".

In Scala, it is also possible for us to use the keyword "*val*" to declare a variable. This is shown below:

val name :String="John"

What we have done is used the keyword "*val*" to declare a variable which we have given the name "*name*". This kind of variable will not change its value. It is called an "*immutable variable*". Trying to change its value will lead to an error.

Variable Data Types

We define the type of our variable after declaring the name of the variable but before the equal sign. Notice that any type of variable can be defined in Scala provided we have mentioned its data type. This can be done as shown below:

valorvalVariable_Name:DataType[=StartValue]

However, it is also possible that we may not want to specify the initial or the start value of the variable which is still valid. This is shown below:

var age :Int;
val name :String;

Inferring the Variable Type

Once an initial value has been assigned to a certain variable the Scala compiler can automatically tell the type of variable that you have declared. This is what is known as *"Variable Type Inference"*. With this, our previous variables can be written as follows:

var age =20;
val name ="John";

With the above declarations, the variable *"age"* will automatically become an integer while the variable *"name"* will automatically become a string.

Multiple Assignments

Multiple assignments are supported in Scala. If a method or a block of code which is expected to return a tuple, then a *"val"* can be assigned to the variable. Consider the example given below:

val(age1:Int,name:String)=Pair(35,"John")

The type reference will still get it right as shown below:

val(age, name)=Pair(35,"John")

Types of Variables

The scope of a variable depends on where it has been declared. There are three different types of scope for variables. These include fields, method parameters or local variables. Let us discuss these briefly.

Fields

These are the type of variables belonging to an object. These variables can be accessed from inside any method which has been declared inside the object. Fields can also be accessed from outside the object in which they have been declared. However, this will depend on the type of access modifier that has been used. Object fields can be declared by use of either the *"val"* or the *"var"* keyword so that they can be either mutable or immutable.

Method Parameters

These are a kind of variables used for passing the values of the arguments or parameters of a particular method whenever the method has been called. Note that these are only accessible from inside the method of declaration. The objects which are being passed in can be accessed from the outside. However, you must have a reference to the object from outside. These are defined by use of the *"val"* keywords and this is why they are always mutable.

Local Variables

These are the variables which have been defined inside a particular method. These can only be accessed from inside that method. However, the created objects can escape the method if they are returned from the method. These can be defined by use of either *"val"* or the *"var"* keyword so as to make them either mutable or immutable.

Chapter 5- Operators in Scala

An operator is just a symbol which tells the Scala compiler to perform a particular mathematical operation or just a logical manipulation. This language has numerous in-built operators including the following:

- Logical Operators

- Assignment Operators

- Arithmetic Operators

- Bitwise Operators

- Relational Operators

Let us discuss these in details.

Arithmetic Operators

These are used to perform various mathematical operations in Scala. They include addition (+), subtraction (-), multiplication (*), division (/) and modulus (%). Let us demonstrate how these are used with a sample program.

Open your text editor and create a new file. Give the file a name with a "*.scala*" extension. Add the following code to the file:

```scala
objectArithmeticTest{
def main(args:Array[String]){
var w =25;
var x=20;
var y=10;
var z=50;
println("x + y = "+(x+ y));
println("x − y = "+(x- y));
println("x * y = "+(x* y));
println("x / y = "+(x/ y));
println("x % y = "+(x% y));
println("z % x = "+(z% x));
}
}
```

Once you have added the above code to your file, save it and the run it. Use the command prompt to navigate to the location of the file and then compile it. After the compilation, execute it. If you do not know how to do this, kindly consult our previous topics. You will observe the following output from the program:

$$x + y = 30$$

$$x - y = 10$$

$$x * y = 200$$

$$x / y = 2$$

$$x \% y = 0$$

$$z \% x = 10$$

You can then see how the mathematical operations have been performed and that they were all successful.

Relational operators

These are mostly used for comparison purposes. Examples of these include the greater than operator (>), less than operator (<), equals operator (==) and many others. Let us demonstrate how these work by use of an example.

Open your text editor and then create a new file. Give the file a name with a "*.scala*" extension and then save it. Add the following code to the file:

```scala
objectRelationTest{
def main(args:Array[String]){
var x =20;
var y =30;
println("x == y = "+(x == y));
println("x != y = "+(x != y));
println("x > y = "+(x > y));
println("x < y = "+(x < y));
println("y >= x = "+(y >= x));
println("y <= x = "+(y <= x));
}
}
```

Once you have added the code, just save the file. You can then run the file. Just use the command prompt to navigate to the directory where it is stored. Compile and then execute the file. You should observe the following output:

x == y = false

x != y = true

x > y = false

x < y = true

y >= x = true

y <= x = false

Bitwise operators

These are the kind of operators which are used to work on the bits by performing a bit by bit operation. They work by first converting the value being passed into bits and then performing operations on them. Let us demonstrate how these work by use of an example.

Just open your text editor and then create a new file. Give it a name ending with a ".*scala*" extension. Save the file and then add the following code to it:

```
objectBitwiseTest{
def main(args:Array[String]){
var x =60;
var y =13;
var z =0;
z = x & y;
println("x & y = "+ z );
z = x | y;
println("x | y = "+ z );
z = x ^ y;
println("x ^ y = "+ z );
z =~x;
println("~x = "+ z );
z = x <<2;
```

```
println("x << 2 = "+ z );
z = x >>2;
println("x >> 2  = "+ z );
z = x >>>2;
println("x >>> 2 = "+ z );
}
}
```

Once you have written the program, just save and then execute it. You should note the following as the output from the program:

$$x \mathbin{\&} y = 12$$

$$x \mid y = 61$$

$$x \mathbin{^\wedge} y = 49$$

$$\sim x = -61$$

$$x \ll 2 = 24(￼$$

$$x \gg 15$$

$$x \ggg 15$$

The output had shown in the above figure shows that our operators worked correctly.

Logical operators

Scala programming language supports a number of logical operators. These include the following:

1. && (logical AND)- the condition is true if both operands are not zero.

2. || (logical OR)- the condition becomes true if any of the operands is not zero.

3. ! (logical NOT)- reverses the logical state of the operand in question. If the condition is true, then this operator will make it false.

Let us demonstrate how these can be used in Scala programming language. Open your text editor and create a new file. Give the file a name ending with a ".*scala*" extension. Save it in a directory where you can easily access. Add the following code to the file:

```
objectLogicalTest {
def main(args: Array[String]) {
var x = true;
var y = false;

println("x && y = " + (x&&y) );

println("x || y = " + (x||y) );

println("!(x && y) = " + !(x && y) );
}
}
```

Once you have added the code just save the file and run it. The following output should be observed from the program:

$$x \ \&\& \ y = false$$

$$x \ || \ y = true$$

$$!(x \ \&\& \ y) = true$$

As shown in the output above, our program has worked effectively. You now know how to use logical operators in Scala programming.

Chapter 6- Decision making in Scala Programming

In Scala programming, decision making statements are highly supported. These help programmers to develop or create programs with the ability to take different actions in different circumstances. Let us discuss these statements.

The "if" statement

This statement takes the following syntax:

if(Boolean_expression)

{

// Statements to be executed when the Boolean expression is true

}

The statements inside the curly braces will be executed if the Boolean expression is found to be true. If the expression is found to be false, then the first statement after the closing curly brace will be executed.Consider the example given below which demonstrates how this statement can be used:

objectIfTest {

```scala
def main(args: Array[String]) {
var a = 20;
if( a<50 ){
println("The if condition is true.");
}
}
}
```

I hope you had created a new file and then saved it with a name with the ".*scala*" extension. Add the code to the file and then execute it. You will notice the following output:

The if condition is true.

The output shows that our Boolean expression was found to be true. Suppose that the Boolean expression as found to be false? Consider the program modified to the following:

```
objectIfTest {
def main(args: Array[String]) {
var a = 100;
if( a < 50 ){
println("The if condition is true.");
}
}
}
```

The Boolean expression above will be found to be false. The reason for this is because the value of the variable "*a*" is not less than 50. Try to run the program and then observe the output that you get. You will get nothing as output. The reason is because we have not specified what is to be done if the condition is found to be false. You will see how to solve this.

The "if...else" statement

This statement is aimed at solving the problem which we discussed in the previous section. It consists of an *"if"* statement and an optional *"else"* statement. The *"else"* statement is executed if the Boolean expression is found to be false. It takes the following syntax:

```
if(Boolean_expression){
//these statements will be executed if the Boolean expression evaluates to //true

}else{
//statements to be executed if the Boolean expression evaluates to false

}
```

Let us demonstrate this by use of an example. Create a new file in your text editor. Give a name with the *".scala"* extension. Add the following code to the file:

```
objectIfElseTest {
def main(args: Array[String]) {
var a = 50;
if( a< 30 ){
println("The Boolean expression is true");
}else{
```

println("The Boolean expression is false");

}

}

}

Once you have added the code to the file, just save it. You can then run the program by following the procedure which we discussed earlier. You will observe the following output from the program:

The Boolean expression is false

The output clearly shows that the Boolean expression was evaluated and found to be false. This is why the last part of the program was executed.

The "if...else if...else" statement

This statement is used if the conditions being tested are numerous. It consists of an "*if*" statement which is followed by an optional "*else if...else*" statement. It takes the following syntax:

if(Boolean_expressiona){

//this will be executed if the expression "*a*" is found to be true.

}else if(Boolean_expressionb){

//this will be executed if the Boolean expression b is found to be true

}else if(Boolean_expressionc){

// this will be executed if the Boolean expression c is found to be true

}else {

//this will be executed if none of the above conditions is met

}

We now need to demonstrate how this statement is used by use of a program. Just open your text editor and then create a new file. Save the file with a name that has a ".*scala*" extension. Add the following code to the file:

```
objectTestProgram {
def main(args: Array[String]) {
var a = 50;
if( a == 20 ){
println("The value of A is 20");
}else if( a == 30 ){
println("The value of A is 30");
}else if( a == 50 ){
println("The value of A is 50");
}else{
println("None of the conditions was met");
}
}
}
```

After adding the code, just save the file and then run it. Observe the output that you get. It should be as follows:

The value of A is 50

The program worked effectively as we have initialized our variable "*a*" to 50. If you modify the value of the variable to either 20 or 30, you will also get the outputs corresponding to those values. However, it is also possible that the value of the variable can be set to something which is not defined in the program. What will happen if the value of the variable is set to 60 as shown below:

```
objectTestProgram {
def main(args: Array[String]) {
var a = 60;
if( a == 20 ){
println("The value of A is 20");
}else if( a == 30 ){
println("The value of A is 30");
}else if( a == 50 ){
println("The value of A is 50");
}else{
println("None of the conditions was met");
}
}
}
```

From what we have in the above program, none of the Boolean expressions will be met. This is where the importance of the "*else*" part will be demonstrated. The statement will be executed and you will notice the following output:

None of the conditions was met

Nested "*if...else*" statement

It is possible for us to nest statements in Scala. In this case, an "*if*" or an "*else if*" statement is used inside another "*if*" or "*else if*" statement. This will take the following syntax:

if(Boolean_expressiona){

//This will be executed if the Boolean expression a is met

if(Boolean_expressionb){
//this will be executed if the Boolean expression b is met

}
}

The above example shows how the "*if*" statement can be nested in Scala. To nest the "*else if...else*" statement in Scala, we use the same syntax shown above. We now want to demonstrate how this can be done by use of an example.

Just open your text editor and then create a new file. Save the file with a name having a ".*scala*" extension. Add the following code to the file:

```
objectTestProgram{
def main(args:Array[String]){
var a =50;
var b =40;
if( a ==50){
if( b ==40){
println("The value of A = 50 and the value of Y = 40");
}
}
}
}
```

After adding the above code, just save the file and then run it. You will notice the following output from the file:

The value of A = 50 and the value of Y = 40

Chapter 7- Loops in Scala

Loops are used when the programmer wants to execute a certain part or block of code in a program a certain number of times. What will happen is that the loop will execute the statements within the block in a sequential manner, that is, the way they are arranged. This means that the execution begins with the first line of code then moves on to the next. There are numerous control structures in Scala programming language which provide programmers with various execution paths.

We will discuss the various types of loops supported in this programming language.

The "while" Loop

This is a kind of loop which will be executed as long as the condition being tested is true. If the test condition becomes false, then the execution of the loop halts. The loop takes the following syntax:

```
while(condition){
statement(s);
}
```

The block can be made of only a single statement or multiple statements. If the condition being tested becomes false, then the execution of the loop is shifted to the line immediately after the closing brace.

The funny thing with this loop is that it might never be executed. Suppose that the test condition is evaluated for the first time and is found to be false, what will happen? The execution will skip to the line immediately after the closing brace. This means that the loop will not be executed even once. Consider the example program given below:

```
objectTestProgram{
def main(args:Array[String]){
// declaring our local variable:
var x=0;
// executing the while loop
while( x<5){
println("The value of x is: "+ x);
x= x+1;
}
}
}
```

Just write the program in your text editor, save and then run it. The program will give the following output:

The value of x is: 0

The value of x is: 1

The value of x is: 2

The value of x is: 3

The value of x is: 4

Notice that the value of the variable "x" has been incrementally increased until it reached four. The last test of the loop found that the value of the variable was five. However, the condition of the loop is that the value of the variable should be less than five. This causes the loop to halt execution immediately. This is why we do not have the value five in the output. That is how the "*while*" loop works.

The "do...while" Loop

With this loop, the test of the conditions isn't done until the end of the loop. This translates to the fact that this loop must be executed at least once when the program is run. Note that we said that the "*while*" loop might never be executed. This, however, is not the case with the loop here. This also marks the difference between the two types of loops.

This loop takes the following syntax in Scala:

do{
statement(s);
}while(condition);

Note the location of the test condition. This makes so that the statements inside the loop will be executed before the test condition is evaluated. If the condition is evaluated to be true, then the execution will jump to the "*do*" at the top of the program. We now need to demonstrate how this works by using an example of the program.

Just open your text editor and create a new file. Give the file a name with a "*.scala*" extension. Save the file and then add the following code to it:

```
objectTestProgram{
def main(args:Array[String]){
// Declaring our local variable:
var x=0;

// executing the do loop
do{
println("The value of x is: "+ x);
x= x+1;
}while( x<5)
}
}
```

Once you have added the code, just run the program and then observe the output. It should be as follows:

```
The value of x is: 0

The value of x is: 1

The value of x is: 2

The value of x is: 3

The value of x is: 4
```

Again, the loop has been executed until it has found to be violating the test condition. Suppose the test condition was found to be false. Let us modify the above program to the following:

```
objectTestProgram{
def main(args:Array[String]){
// Declaring our local variable:
var x =50;

// executing the do loop
do{
println("The value of x is: "+ x );
x = x +1;
}while( x <5)
}
}
```

The value of variable "x" should be less than five but we have initialized it at fifty. Just run the program and observe the output. It will be as follows:

The value of x is: 50

The reason for the above output is that the loop was executed once before the test condition was evaluated.

The "for" Loops

This type of loop lets the programmer execute part of the code a certain number of times. The number of times the loop is to be executed is always specified inside the loop. This loop takes various forms which we will discuss in this chapter.

"for" Loop with Ranges

It is the simplest "*for* " loop which is supported in Scala and it takes the following syntax:

for(var a <- Range){
statement(s);
}

The "*Range*" in this case is in terms of numbers starting from "*i*" to "*j*". The operator used above, that is, (<-) will generate the numbers from the range that you have specified and this is why it is called the "*generator*". Let us demonstrate this by use of an example.

Just open your text editor and then create a new file. Give it a name with a "*.scala*" extension. Save the file and then add the following code to it:

```
objectTestProgram {
def main(args: Array[String]) {
var x = 0;
// executing a "for" loop with a range
for( x<- 1 to 5){
println( "The value of x is: " + x );
}
}
}
```

Just save the program after adding the above code and then run it. You will observe the following output:

```
The value of x is: 1

The value of x is: 2

The value of x is: 3

The value of x is: 4

The value of x is: 5
```

As shown in the above figure, the range for the values is between one and five, and this is what we specified in the code. The syntax used if "*i to j*". We now need to demonstrate how we can use the "*i until j*" syntax to get our output. Consider the example given below:

```
objectTestProgram {
def main(args: Array[String]) {
var x = 0;
// for loop execution with a range
for( x <- 1 until 5){
println( "The value of x is: " + x );
}
}
}
```

Once you have written the program, just save the file; don't forget the "*.scala*" extension. You can then run it and you will observe the following output:

The value of x is: 1

The value of x is: 2

The value of x is: 3

The value of x is: 4

As shown in the above figure which represents the output, the last value of the range is not part of the output. You are now aware of the difference between the two types of loops.

If you need to use multiple ranges in your loop, separate them by use of a semicolon. With this, all cases of the ranges which are possible will be iterated. Let's see an example involving only two ranges to demonstrate their use, note that you can have more than 2 of these. Just create a new file and the save it. The name should have the ".*scala*" extension. Add the following code to the file:

```
objectTestProgram {
def main(args: Array[String]) {
var x = 0;
var y = 0;
```

```
// executing a for loop having a range
for( x <- 1 to 3; y <- 1 to 3){
println( "The value of x: " + x );
println( "The value of y: " + y );
}
}
}
```

Once you have written the above program, just save and then execute it. You will get the following output:

The value of x: 1

The value of y: 1

The value of x: 1

The value of y: 2

The value of x: 1

The value of y: 3

The value of x: 2

The value of y: 1

The value of x: 2

The value of y: 2

The value of x: 2

The value of y: 3

The value of x: 3

The value of y: 1

The value of x: 3

The value of y: 2

The value of x: 3

The value of y: 3

Our program has worked effectively as shown in the above figure which represents the output from the program.

"for" Loop with Collections

This type of "for" loop takes the following syntax:

```
for(var a <- List ){
statement(s);
}
```

The "List" in this case is a list containing the elements which the loop is to iterate. At each iteration, a single element which is in "a" will be returned by the loop. Consider the example given below:

```
objectTestProgram {
def main(args: Array[String]) {
var x = 0;
valmyList = List(11,12,13,14,15);
// executing a "for"loop with a collection
for( a <- numList ){
println( "The value of x is: " + x );
}
}
```

```
}
```

Just save the program above and then execute it. You will note the following output:

The value of x: 11

The value of x: 12

The value of x: 13

The value of x: 14

The value of x: 15

The program has worked effectively as shown in the above output.

"for" Loop with Filters

With this loop, programmers can use the "*if*" statement to filter one or more elements which have been specified. This loop takes the following syntax:

```
for(var a<- List
ifcondition_a; ifcondition_b...
){
statement(s);
}
```

If you need to use several filters for the expression, use a semicolon to separate them. Let us demonstrate the use of this loop with an example:

```
objectTestProgram {
def main(args: Array[String]) {
var x = 0;
valmyList = List(11,12,13,14,15,16,17,18,19,20);
// executing a for loop having multiple filters.
for( x <- myList
if x != 13; if x < 18 ){
println( "The value of x is: " + x );
}
}
```

}

Just save the program and then run it. Observe the output that you get which should be as follows:

The value of x is: 11

The value of x is: 12

The value of x is: 14

The value of x is: 15

The value of x is: 16

The value of x is: 17

You can now see the output as shown in the above figure. The number thirteen is not part of the output since we used the operator "!" which indicates that it should not be included in the output. The output does not go beyond seventeen since we specified it should be less than eighteen.

"for" Loop with Yield

The values which are to be returned from a *"for"* loop can be stored in either a function or in a variable. This can be done by using the prefix *"yield"* before the *"for"* loop expression, which is shown below:

varrVal=for{var a <-List
ifcondition_a;ifcondition_b...
}yield a

Notice the use of the curly braces in our program to store the variables and the conditions. The variable *"rValue"* was used to store the values of the variable *"a"* in the form of a collection. We now need to demonstrate how to use the *"for"* loop with *"yield"* in a program.

Just open your text editor and then create a new file. The name should have a "*.scala*" extension. Add the following code to the file:

```scala
objectTestProgram{
def main(args:Array[String]){
var x =0;
valmyList=List(11,12,13,14,15,16,17,18,19,20);
// ececuting the "for" loop with a yield
varrVal=for{ x<-myList
if x!=3;ifx<8
}yield x
// using another loop to print the values having been returned.
for( x<-rVal){
println("The value of x is: "+ x);
}
}
}
```

Once you have written the above program, just save the file and then execute the program. You will observe the following output from the program:

The value of x is: 11

The value of x is: 12

The value of x is: 14

The value of x is: 15

The value of x is: 16

The value of x is: 17

The number thirteen is not part of the output because this is what we have instructed the program to do. The outputted numbers do not exceed the number seventeen since they were specified to be less than eighteen. The outputs above demonstrate that the program has worked.

Chapter 8- Functions in Scala

A function is made up of a group of statements which are put together to perform a particular task. A program code can be divided into separate functions. You can do this any way you'd like, but it ultimately depends on the purpose of each function as they are used to perform a specific task. Scala programming language supports both functions and methods which are closely related with only a minor difference.

We can define a program anywhere within a Scala program. It is also possible for us to define functions which are nested. The name of the function can even include some of the special symbols such as +, /,* and others.

Function Declaration

To declare functions in Scala, we follow the syntax shown below:

deffunction_Name([list of arguments/parameters]):[return type]

If an equal sign and the method body are not specified, then the method is declared as abstract.

Function Definition

To define functions, we use the following syntax:

deffunctionName([list of arguments]):[return type]={

function body
return[expression]
}

The return type in this case can be of any type provided it is a valid datum within Scala. The arguments are separated by a comma if there are more than one. However, these and the return type are optional. Consider the function given below:

objectaddNum{

```
defaddInt( x:Int, y:Int):Int={
varsum:Int=0
sum= x + y
return sum
}
}
```

When this function is executed, it will return the sum of two variables, "*X*" and "*Y*". You are aware of void functions in Java, which are the functions which do not return anything. In Scala, these types of functions are called "*procedures*". Procedures are declared as follows in Scala:

```
objectSalutation{
defprintHello():Unit={
println("Hello there!")
}
}
```

Calling Functions

There are numerous ways to invoke or call functions in Scala. The following is the syntax for calling functions in Scala:

functionName(list of parameters)

Let us demonstrate how to define and call a function by use of an example:

```
objectTestProgram{
def main(args:Array[String]){
println("The returned Value is: "+addInt(8,9));
}
defaddInt( x:Int, y:Int):Int={
varsum:Int=0
sum= x + y
return sum
}
}
```

Just write the above program and then run it. You will observe the following output:

The returned Value is: 17

Chapter 9- Closures in Scala

A closure is a special kind of a function. The return value of a closure is determined by one or more variables which have been declared outside the function. Consider the anonymous function given below:

valanswer=(j:Int)=> j * 5

In the above code, we have used only one variable. It has been defined as a parameter of the code. Now consider the code given below:

val answer =(j:Int)=> j * number

This time, we have defined two variables, that is, "*j*" and "*number*". The first variable, that is, "j", has been used formally in the function. Whenever the "*answer*" is called, this variable will be bound to a new value. Note that the variable "*number*" has not been defined formally in the function. Consider the code given below:

varnumber=3
valanswer=(j:Int)=> j*number

In the above code, the variable *"number"* has a reference which has been defined outside the function. Consider the example given below:

```
objectTestProgram{
def main(args:Array[String]){
println("answer(1) value = "+ answer(1))
println("answer(2) value = "+ answer(2))
}
var number =3
val answer =(j:Int)=> j * number
}
```

Just write the program as it is shown and then run it. You will observe the following output:

answer(1) value = 3

answer(2) value = 6

The function will reference the variable *"number"* each time *"answer"* is called.

Chapter 10- Strings in Scala

Consider the example given below:

objectTestProgram{
valsalutation:String="Hello there!"
def main(args:Array[String]){
println(salutation)
}
}

We have used the keyword *"val"* to define a variable and then we have assigned a string to it. We have used the value of the type *"java.lang.string"* which has been borrowed from Java. Note that Scala strings are immutable, that is, they cannot be modified.

There are two ways strings can be defined. These are shown below:

var salutation ="Hello there!";
or
varsalutation:String="Hello there!";

When a compiler encounters a string literal during compilation, it creates an string type object. A value is also associated to this object. You can also use the *"String"* keyword for this purpose. Consider the example shown below:

```
objectTestProgram{
val salutation:String="Hello there!"
def main(args:Array[String]){
println( salutation )
}
}
```

Just write the program and then run it. You will observe the following output:

Hello there!

String Length

Accessor methods are used to obtain information about a particular object. *"length()"* is one of the accessor methods which can be applied on a particular string. This method, when used, returns the number of characters which are used on a particular string object. Consider the example given below:

```
objectTestProgram{
def main(args:Array[String]){
varmyString="Scala is interesting";
var length =myString.length();
println("The length of the string is: "+ length );
}
}
```

Just write the above program and then run it. You will observe the following output:

The length of the string is: 5

Concatenation of Strings

In Scala, there is a method for us to concatenate or join strings. This is demonstrated below:

String_a.concat(string_b);

The composite string will be made up of the first string followed by the second string which has been joined together. The method can also be used together with String literals. This is shown below:

"I am ".concat("John");

In most cases, the "+" operator is used to concatenate strings. This can be used as follows:

"Hello"+" there"+"!"

Consider the example given below which illustrates how concatenation of strings can be done:

```
objectTestProgram{
def main(args:Array[String]){
var string1 =" is easy ";
var string2 ="It is very useful";
```

```
    println("Scala "+ string1 + string2);
}
}
```

Just write the above program, save it and then run it. You will observe the following output:

Scala is easy It is very useful

Format strings

The *"printf"* and *"format()"* methods can be used to give the output while formatted. Consider the following example:

```
objectTestProgram{
def main(args:Array[String]){
varfVar=17.96
variVar=4500
varsVar="Hello there!"
var f =printf("The float variable has value "+
"%f, while the integer variable has value "+
"variable is %d, and the string is "+
"is %s",fVar,iVar,sVar)
println(f)
}
}
```

Just write the program as shown above, save it and then run it. You will observe the following output:

The float variable has value 17.96,while

the integer variable has value 4500, and the

string is Hello there!

Conclusion

It can be concluded that Scala is a very useful programming language. The language's constructs are closely related to those of Java programming language, thus, Java experts find it easy to learn this programming language. Those who are comfortable with other programming languages such as C, C++, and Python also learn this language's constructs very easily. To begin the process of programming in Scala programming language, you need to begin by setting up the environment.

Java needs to be set up correctly, including the environment variable and the PATH variable. You can then download and install Scala itself. The programming language is supported on various operating systems including Windows, Linux and Mac OS X. This shows how diverse the language is.

The language has a strong support for variables. There are two keywords which can be used for variable declaration and these determine whether the variable is mutable or immutable. Mutable variables are the ones which can be changed while immutable are the ones which cannot be changed. The programmer can then choose between these two depending on what they need or expect.

The language also has a string support for operators of different types, including arithmetic operators, logical operators, assignment operators and others. With decision making statements in Scala, you can be able to write programs with the ability to evaluate different conditions and then take the necessary action. Loops of various types are also supported in this programming language. My hope is that this book has helped you to learn most concepts associated with this programming language.

Thank you!

We would like to thank you for buying this book. Hope you found it helpful in your now EASY and FAST programming life development. And we are happy to recommend you some other books from this author:

ANDROID PROGRAMMING: Complete Introduction for Beginners -Step By Step Guide How to Create Your Own Android App Easy!

ANDROID GAME PROGRAMMING: COMPLETE INTRODUCTION FOR BEGINNERS: STEP BY STEP GUIDE HOW TO CREATE YOUR OWN ANDROID APP EASY!

Linux Command Line: FAST and EASY! (Linux Commands, Bash Scripting Tricks, Linux Shell Programming Tips and Bash One-Liners)

**Linux Command Line: Become a Linux Expert!
(Input/Output Redirection, Wildcards, File Security,
Processes Managing, Shell Programming Advanced
Features, GUI elements, Useful Linux Commands)**

PHP and MySQL Programming for Beginners: A Step by Step Course From Zero to Professional

Python Programming: Getting started FAST With Learning of Python Programming Basics in No Time.

DOCKER: Everything You Need to Know to Master Docker (Docker Containers, Linking Containers, Whalesay Image, Docker Installing on Mac OS X and Windows OS)

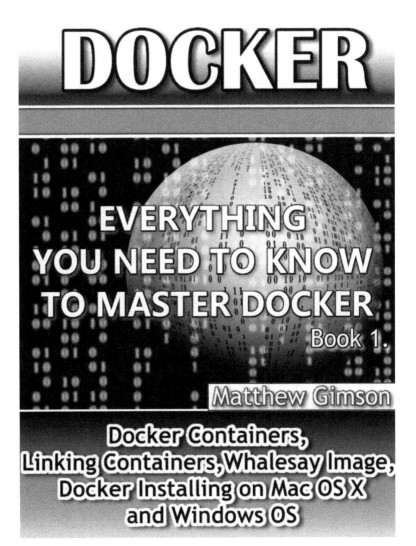

Docker: Docker Guide for Production Environment
(Programming is Easy Book 8)

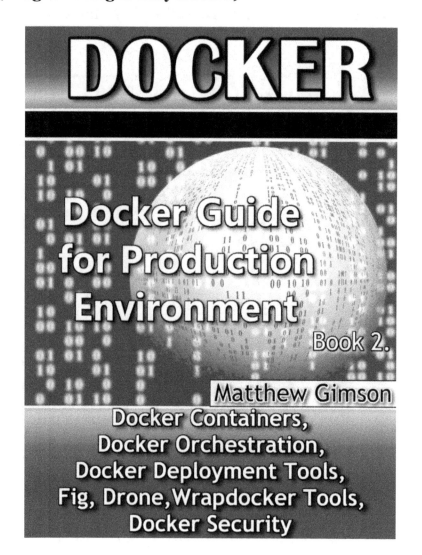

Excel VBA Programming: Learn Excel VBA Programming FAST and EASY! (Programming is Easy Book 9)

VAGRANT: Make Your Life Easier With VAGRANT. Master VAGRANT FAST and EASY! (Programming is Easy Book 10)